Nichole's Book of Practical Things

RACHEL BARNARD

Doughnut image from "FreeImages.com/ Erik Araujo."

Book cover artist: SelfPubBookCovers.com/VISIONS

ISBN-10: 1944022058
ISBN-13: 978-1944022051

CONTENTS

KITCHEN HACKS

Take the quiz!

How well do you know your way around the kitchen? Take this quiz to find out.

1. Can you convert the following measurements?
   a. 16 Tbsp. = x cups?
   b. 1 Gallon = x cups?
   c. 1 lb. = x ounces?
2. Do you know the minimum cooking temperatures for beef, pork, poultry, and fish?
3. Can you make a pancake from scratch?
4. Do you know how to boil an egg?
5. Do you know how to cook rice without under or over cooking it?

If you answered yes to all the above (and were able to do the conversions), congratulations, you are adulting quite well! If you answered no to several or all, never fear, this book and the mighty powers of google will be able to help you out.

Kitchen Hacks

Making a pie crust from scratch

INGREDIENTS

- 2 1/2 cups all-purpose flour
- 1 teaspoon salt
- 1 teaspoon sugar
- 2 sticks chilled unsalted butter, cut into pieces

DIRECTIONS

1. To make the dough for the pie crust, mix 2 ½ cups all-purpose flour and 1 teaspoon each salt and sugar in a medium-size bowl. Cut 2 sticks chilled unsalted butter into pieces. With a pastry blender, cut in butter, working until mixture resembles coarse meal.

2. Add 4 tablespoons ice water; work with hands until dough comes together. If dough is still crumbly, add more ice water a tablespoon at a time (up to 4 more tablespoons). Do not overwork.

3. Divide dough in half, and flatten halves into disks. Wrap disks separately in plastic; refrigerate at least 1 hour.

4. To form the pie shell, roll the dough on a floured surface into a 14-inch round. Wrap around rolling pin and carefully unroll over a 9-inch pie plate.

5. Fit gently into bottom and side of plate. Use kitchen shears to trim dough to a 1-inch overhang; fold under, and seal to form a rim.

6. Crimp rim with fingertips and knuckle. Repeat with remaining dough; wrap each with plastic, stack, and freeze.

Kitchen Hacks

Simple recipes

Hummus

Blend together the following ingredients: 1 clove garlic, 1 can chickpeas, 4 tbsp. lemon juice, 2 tbsp. tahini, 1 tsp. salt, 2 tbsp. olive oil. Transfer the mixture to a medium serving bowl. Sprinkle with pepper and pour olive oil over the top.

Guacamole

Mix together the following ingredients: 2 avocados, ½ tsp. salt, 1 tbsp. lime juice, 2 tbsp. of minced onion, 2 tbsp. chopped cilantro, dash of black pepper, ½ chopped tomato.

Pancake Mix

Mix together the following ingredients: 1 cup all-purpose flour, 2 tbsp. white sugar, 2 tsp. baking powder, 1 tsp. salt, 1 beaten egg, 1 cup milk, 2 tbsp. vegetable oil.

Pizza Dough

Pour 1 ½ cups warm water into a large bowl and sprinkle in 2 packets of active dry yeast. Let stand until foamy (5 minutes). Whisk 2 tbsp. sugar, ¼ cup oil, and 2 tsp. salt into yeast mixture. Add 4 cups all-purpose flour until a sticky dough forms. Transfer dough to an oiled bowl and brush top with oil. Cover bowl with plastic wrap and set aside in a warm, draft-free place until dough has doubled in bulk, about 1 hour. Turn out onto a lightly floured work surface and gently knead 1 or 2 times before using.

Omelet

Beat 2 eggs, 2 tbsp. water, dash of salt, and a dash of pepper in a small bowl until blended. Heat 1 tsp. butter in a nonstick skillet over medium-high heat until hot. Tilt pan to coat bottom. Pour in egg mixture. When top surface of eggs is thickened and no visible liquid egg remains, fold omelet in half with a spatula then slide omelet onto plate and serve immediately.

Mac n' Cheese

Bring a large pot of lightly salted water to boil. Cook 1 box of elbow macaroni in the boiling water, stirring occasionally until it's cooked through but firm (8 minutes). Drain. Melt ¼ cup butter in the same pot over medium heat. Stir in ¼ cup all-purpose flour, ½ tsp. salt, dash of black pepper for about 5 minutes. Slowly pour 2 cups milk into mixture while continuously stirring until mixture is smooth (5 minutes). Add 2 cups shredded cheddar cheese until it's melted (3 minutes). Fold macaroni into cheese sauce until coated.

Chocolate Chip Cookies

Preheat oven to 375° F. Combine 2 ¼ cups all-purpose flour, 1 tsp. baking soda, and 1 tsp. salt in a small bowl. Beat 1 cup (2 sticks) butter, ¾ cup granulated sugar, ¾ cup brown sugar, and 1 tsp. vanilla extract in a large bowl until creamy. Add 2 eggs, one at a time, beating well. Gradually beat in flour mixture. Stir in 2 cups of semi-sweet chocolate chips. Form into balls and place onto ungreased baking sheets (12 per sheet). Bake for 9-11 minutes or until golden brown. Cool before eating.

Kitchen Hacks

Conversion chart

MEASURE	EQUIVALENT
1/16 teaspoon	dash
1/8 teaspoon	a pinch
3 teaspoons	1 Tablespoon
1/8 cup	2 tablespoons (= 1 standard coffee scoop)
1/4 cup	4 Tablespoons
1/3 cup	5 Tablespoons plus 1 teaspoon
1/2 cup	8 Tablespoons
3/4 cup	12 Tablespoons
1 cup	16 Tablespoons
1 Pound	16 ounces
US liquid volume measurements	
8 Fluid ounces	1 Cup
1 Pint	2 Cups (= 16 fluid ounces)
1 Quart	2 Pints (= 4 cups)
1 Gallon	4 Quarts (= 16 cups)
US to Metric Conversions	
1/5 teaspoon	1 ml (ml stands for milliliter, one thousandth of a liter)
1 teaspoon	5 ml
1 tablespoon	15 ml
1 fluid oz.	30 ml
1/5 cup	50 ml
1 cup	240 ml
2 cups (1 pint)	470 ml
4 cups (1 quart)	.95 liter
4 quarts (1 gal.)	3.8 liters
1 oz.	28 grams
1 pound	454 grams

Kitchen Hacks

Food and kitchen safety

Whether you work in a restaurant or cook food at home, here are some tips for staying safe and far away from food poisoning!

- Poultry should always be cooked until the minimum temperature is 165° F.
- The danger zone for biological growth in food is defined as 41 degrees F to 140° F.
- Food should not be kept in the danger zone for more than 4 hours.
- Proper food contact surface is stainless steel.
- In a kitchen refrigerator, the following order is an acceptable order to store goods, listed from lowest point in the refrigerator to the highest point: poultry, meat, vegetables.
- The cooking temperature for raw pork is 145° F.
- An opened package of hot dogs should be used for no more than 1 week.
- Your refrigerator should be kept at a maximum temperature of 40 degrees F at all times.
- You should not defrost frozen meat on your countertop, but you can defrost in the microwave, in the refrigerator, or by running in cold water.
- Strawberries are a potentially hazardous food.
- The minimum cooking temperature for foods containing raw eggs is 160° F.
- Foods can hold in the refrigerator above 41° F for up to 2 hours before you should throw them away.
- Use a different cutting board for meats & vegetables.
- The cold storage time for ground beef in a refrigerator set to 40° F or below is 1-2 days.

Kitchen Hacks

Kitchen lingo

Al dente – Food (typically pasta) cooked so it's still firm.

Baste – To pour juices or melted fat over meat during cooking in order to keep it moist.

Blanch – Typically a vegetable or fruit scalded in boiling water for a brief timed interval and then plunged into iced water or cold running water to halt the cooking process.

Broil – To cook meat or fish with direct & intense radiant heat.

Dredge – To coat wet or moist foods with a dry ingredient prior to cooking.

Fillet – To remove the bones from a fish.

Flambé – To cover food with liquor and set alight briefly.

Julienne – To cut food into thin strips/small match like pieces.

Pare – To cut off the outer layer using a sharp knife.

Pinch – Precisely 1/8 tsp. The amount that can be taken between the thumb and forefinger.

Poach – To cook by submerging food in a liquid (using a relatively low temperature).

Reduce – To thicken and intensify the flavor of a liquid by simmering or boiling.

Render – To melt and clarify hard animal fat for cooking purposes.

Scald – To heat (usually milk) to a point where it's just about to boil. Small bubbles will start to appear around the edges.

Simmer – To cook foods in hot liquids just below the boiling point of water.

CAR HACKS

Take the quiz!

How well do you know your car? Take this quiz to find out.

1. Can you pump your own gas?
2. Do you know how to check your oil?
3. Do you know how to check your tire pressure?
4. Do you know how to jumpstart your car?
5. Do you still have your car's manual handy?
6. Do you know how to change a tire?
7. Do you have AAA?
8. Can you drive a stick shift/manual?
9. Can you find your way around without a GPS/phone?
10. Do you have a roadside emergency bag?

If you answered yes to all the above, congratulations, you are adulting quite well! If you answered no to several or all, never fear, this book and the mighty powers of google will be able to help you out.

Car Hacks

Pumping your own gas

1. Park with your gas tank opening next to the pump and turn off your car.
2. To pay at the pump, slide your card and follow the instructions. To pre-pay (cash or card), go inside and tell the attendant which pump you are parked. If you want to fill up your tank, overpay, and then return after pumping to get your change.
3. Remove the gas cap from your car and set it somewhere safe so you don't forget it.
4. Remove the gas nozzle and insert it into your gas tank opening. Push it until it sits snugly. Be careful to choose the regular or diesel nozzle if there are two nozzles. The pump nozzle should fit snuggle into your gas tank without you having to hold it.
5. Select the correct grade – regular, mid-grade, or premium. Check your owner's manual if you're unsure. For most car's, regular is fine. Make your selection by pressing the corresponding button on the pump. Sometimes, the gas pump sits in a seat where you have to flip it up before you can pump your gas.
6. Some pumps you'll have to press start before pumping.
7. Squeeze the trigger on the pump to activate the gas. On most pumps you can lock the trigger.
8. Most machines will stop the flow of gas when your tank is full. You'll hear a click when the tank is full or when the machine cuts it off.
9. Remove and replace the nozzle in the pump seat of the machine and push the seat back down if need be.
10. Recap your gas tank – twisting until it clicks.
11. Accept or reject the receipt or get your change from the attendant.

Car Hacks

Checking your oil

1. Park on level ground.
2. Your engine should be off and cold.
3. Open the car's hood and find the dipstick.
4. Pull the dipstick out from the engine and wipe any oil off of it with a paper towel.
5. Insert the dipstick back into its tube and push it all the way back in.
6. Pull the dipstick back out and look at both sides to see where the oil is on the end.
7. The dipstick should indicate high and low measurements.
8. If the top of the oil is between the two marks or within the crosshatched area, the level is fine.
9. If the oil is below the minimum mark, add oil.
10. If the oil's color is black or brown, that's fine. But if it's a light, milky color, this could mean coolant is leaking into the engine. Look closely for any metal particles, as this could mean there's internal engine damage. If either of these conditions exist, you should go to a mechanic for further diagnosis or have the car towed.
11. Wipe off the dipstick again and insert it back into its tube, making sure its fully seated.
12. Close the hood.
13. To add oil: refer to your owner's manual for the oil you will need. Remove the oil filler cap and add oil a little at a time (starting with half a quart). Using a funnel helps avoid spills. Wait a minute and check the dipstick again. If the level is still low, add the rest of the quart. Unless your engine is leaking, burning oil, or you haven't checked it in a while, you will rarely need to add more than a quart. Screw the oil filler cap back on securely.

Car Hacks

Checking your tire pressure

1. Find your car owner's manual and look up 'tires' to find the front and rear "PSI" listings.
2. PSI = pounds per square inch and is how you can tell if your tires are properly inflated.
3. Hot or cold temperatures, driving distance, and towing weight can affect tire pressure.
4. The recommendation is to check your tire pressure each month, especially as temperatures heat up.
5. You will need an accurate tire pressure gauge (battery-operated digital gauge or stick-type gauge).
6. Remove the end caps on your tires' air valves (don't lose them!).
7. Place the tire pressure gauge into the valve stem and press down quickly to get a reading.
8. Check the PSI reading and compare to your car's recommended PSI.
9. Take a few readings to eliminate anomalies.
10. If the reading is above the recommendation, push in the valve to let out some air.
11. If the reading is below the recommendation, fill your tire with air until you reach the ideal level.

Car Hacks

Jumpstarting your car

1. Caution: if either car has an electronic ignition system or is an alternatively fueled car, jumper cables may cause damage!
2. Take out your jumper cables (a good item to keep in your emergency roadside kit!)
3. Place both cars in Park or Neutral and shut off the ignition in both cars. Engage both parking brakes.
4. Attach one of the red clips to the POSITIVE terminal of your battery (indicated by POS or + or the bigger terminal)
5. Attach the other red clip to the POSITIVE terminal of the other car.
6. Attach one of the black clips to the NEGATIVE terminal on the OTHER battery.
7. Attach the last black clip to an unpainted metal surface on your car that isn't near the battery.
8. Start the working car and let the engine run for a few minutes.
9. Try to start your own car. If it won't start, make sure the cables are properly connected and have the OTHER car run their engine for five minutes. Try to start your car again. If it still won't start, your battery is probably too dead to revive.
10. If your car starts, congrats on adulting! Remember to keep your engine running and drive around for at least 15 minutes to recharge your battery.
11. If your car won't start the next time you use it, the battery isn't holding a charge and needs to be replaced.

Car Hacks

Changing your car's tire

1. You will need your owner's manual, a spare tire, lug wrench, jack, and your adulating skills.
2. For flats while driving, move your car slowly to a straight, level stretch of road with a wide shoulder.
3. Put on your hazards
4. Apply the parking brake
5. Apply wheel wedges (to the front of the front tires if changing a rear tire and behind the rear tires if changing a front tire).
6. Remove the hubcap or wheel cover unless your lug nuts are exposed. Use the flat end of te lug wrench to remove the hubcap.
7. Loosen the lug nuts, but don't remove completely.
8. Place the jack under the car beneath the frame alongside the flat tire. Follow owner manual instructions for placement.
9. Raise the car with the jack 6" off the ground. (a 2x6" piece of wood beneath the jack prevents settling).
10. Fully unscrew the lug nuts.
11. Remove the flat tire.
12. Mount the spare tire on the lug bolts.
13. Tighten the lug nuts by hand.
14. Lower the car until it just touches the ground and tighten the lug nuts again with the wrench (push down on the wrench using your body weight).
15. Lower the car completely and remove the jack. Tighten the lug nuts again with the wrench.
16. Replace the hubcap.
17. Check the tire pressure.

Car Hacks

Tips for driving a manual car

1. Practice shifting gears and pressing the clutch and gas while the car is off.
2. To start the car, press in the clutch and brake and turn the key.
3. Don't switch gears without fully depressing the clutch pedal
4. Make sure the gear is fully engaged when shifting.
5. If the engine is making a dying animal sound, you're probably in too low a gear and you need to upshift. If the engine is rumbling like a storm, you're probably in too a high a gear and you need to downshift.
6. Don't rest your foot on the clutch pedal when you're in gear.
7. To come to a stop – press on the clutch and shift to neutral before removing your foot from the clutch pedal and coasting or braking to a stop.
8. You can use the emergency brake when starting from a stop on a hill!
9. Set your emergency brake every time you park on a hill and remember... turn your front wheels so that if your car starts rolling (gasp) it would roll into the sidewalk and not into traffic.

Car Hacks

Your roadside emergency bag

1. Owner's Manual
2. Flashlight with working batteries
3. Rain poncho
4. Small cut of 2" x 6" wood to secure a jack
5. Gloves
6. Wheel wedges
7. Jack
8. Lug wrench
9. Spare tire
10. Tire pressure gauge
11. Jumper cables
12. Tissues, paper towels
13. First aid kit
14. Road flares
15. Tarp
16. Rags
17. Duct tape
18. Non-perishable snacks
19. Ice scraper
20. Multipurpose tools
21. Cash
22. Tow rope
23. Compass
24. Safety vest
25. Emergency whistle
26. Cable ties
27. AAA membership

LIFE HACKS

Take the quiz!

How well can you do the following?

1. Negotiate a raise
2. Craft a new resume
3. Interview
4. Barter
5. Use chopsticks
6. Do laundry
7. Write a letter
8. Write a check
9. Get out a stain?
10. How much to tip
11. Treat a bug bite

If you answered yes to all the above, congratulations, you are adulting quite well! If you answered no to several or all, never fear, this book and the mighty powers of google will be able to help you out.

Life Hacks

Tips for negotiating a raise

1. Timing – It's a great time to ask for a raise after you have a track record of accomplishments or if you've done something exceptional. Don't ask for a raise if you just got hired or if the company is struggling financially. Don't wait until review time, but start conversations about raises 3-4 months in advance.
2. A raise shouldn't be based on personal reasons, but on merit and value at your job.
3. Know your worth. Look up similar job salaries.
4. Don't salary compare with others at the same company.
5. Bring details to support your case – monies earned, value raised, recent accomplishments and influence on the company.
6. Be amenable to them saying no and don't assume you're going to get the raise.
7. Rehearse what you're going to say ahead of time – practice with a friend or loved one.
8. Don't leave empty handed – you can always negotiate for other benefits such as training, vacation days, or other perks.
9. Be respectful and mind what you say.
10. Don't rush to fill the silences – stay calm.
11. Set the meeting for Thursday.
12. Be confident.
13. If asking for an amount – be specific, don't give a range.
14. Keep negotiating – don't give up and just accept the first offer.

Life Hacks

Interview Tips

1. Dress the part!
2. Remember to say thank you at the end.
3. Practice answering interview questions.
4. ~~Stalk~~ Research your employer and the business.
5. Be on time.
6. Stay calm.
7. Clean up your social media so ghosts and skeletons don't keep you from your dream job.
8. Be aware of your body language.
9. Bring a few questions about the position or company to ask.
10. Don't get too chummy – be professional.
11. Acknowledge your weaknesses.
12. Be memorable.
13. Follow up.

Life Hacks

Bartering Tips

1. Figure out what you have to offer.
2. Just ask… "How about a trade?"
3. Figure out the dollar value of your goods or services.
4. Put it in writing.
5. Sometimes you are required to report bartering on your taxes as it can be considered income!
6. Be safe: barter in a public place and bring a buddy if you can.
7. Don't bring cash.
8. Put on your poker face.
9. Be wary of scams.
10. Be polite, professional, and patient.
11. Test items to make sure they work.
12. Add something extra if you can't come to an agreement with the other person.
13. For a bartered service, agree on a deadline for completion.
14. The Boot is something you throw in to make a trade equal for both parties.
15. A horse trader is someone who has a real knack for setting up deals with three or more people. Taking into account what people are offering and what they are seeking in return and putting forth a deal that will solve all of their needs.
16. Things you can barter with or get from bartering: haircuts, massages, phones, computers, clothing, toys, books, gifts, crafts.

Life Hacks

Laundry Tips

1. Use a mesh bag for socks to keep any from wandering off.
2. To prevent sneakers from banging around, wedge the knotted together laces in the dryer door.
3. Wash dark clothes inside out to prevent fading.
4. Soak stains immediately.
5. Don't overstuff.
6. Add soap before the clothes.
7. Use ice cubes in the dryer to get rid of wrinkles.
8. Mark your measuring cup.
9. Clean your machine and vacuum your dryer.
10. Remove stains from whites with lemon juice and sunshine.
11. You can make your own laundry detergent and fabric softener.
12. Leave the leather and suede to the professionals.
13. Avoid pressure and direct heat when dealing with stains.
14. You can use vinegar to soften tough fabrics.
15. Use chalk to get out grease stains.

Life Hacks

Writing letters

1. Use a standard font and size (Ariel or Times New Roman for business letters and font size 10-12).
2. Never handwrite a business letter.
3. Your first letter is always a draft.
4. Allow for revision time and thinking things over.
5. Be clear and easy to understand.
6. Always check your spelling and proof-read.

Sample Friendly Letter

March 31, 2017

Dear Readers

How are you? I'm really glad you're reading this and hope you get a chance to read my For the Love of Donuts Books.

I created this accompaniment book for Nichole and all the Nichole's out there (we all have a little bit of Nichole in us) who want to adult, but might be a little confused how to adult successfully. I learned some neat tricks from organizing this book and am glad to share them with you.

Love,
Rachel

Life Hacks

Tips for Tipping

1. Generally tips in the USA are between 15%-20%. Federal minimum wage is approximately $7.25/hour, while employers are legally allowed to pay wages as low as $2.13/hour. Tipping etiquette differs per state.
2. Food (to be calculated pre-sales tax).
    a. 15%-20% for sit down restaurants.
    b. 10% for servers at a buffet.
    c. $1 to $2 per drink for bartenders.
    d. A couple dollars for pizza delivery.
    e. To indicate dissatisfaction with service – leave 2 pennies side by side on top of the tipped bills or by themselves.
3. Travel
    a. Valet – $3-$5
    b. Taxi drivers – 15%-20%
    c. Hotel staff - $2 to $5 per night with a thank you note
    d. Bellhops and skycaps - $2 for the first bag and $1 for each additional bag.
    e. Doorman - $1-$2 to carry luggage or hail a cab.
4. Beauty
    a. Spa – massage or other treatment – 10%--20% (some spas include the tip in the bill).
    b. Hairdresser/manicurist – 10%--20%
5. Miscellaneous
    a. Dealers – 5% of the bet amount at the end of the session.
    b. Tour guides – 15%-20% or more.

Life Hacks

Small medical issues home remedies

1. Bug bites and stings
   a. Essential oils all have properties that can alleviate itching, pain, and swelling. Tea tree oil is antibacterial.
   b. Honey is an anti-inflammatory.
   c. Milk and water combined in equal parts to dab at the skin and soothe it (good for sunburn too).
   d. Lemon or lime can help with itching and are antibacterial.
   e. Toothpaste with menthol will cool and soothe the skin as well as reduce swelling.
   f. Basil leaves soothe the skin (crush and apply bits directly).
   g. Ice can alleviate itching.
   h. Tea bags can draw out the fluid of a bite to reduce itching and swelling.
   i. Vinegar can reduce itching.
   j. For a sting: Remove the stinger. Remain calm. Elevate the limb. See a doctor for scorpion stings.
2. Cuts – for relief, you can use one of the following for relief:
   a. Superglue
   b. Honey
   c. Garlic
   d. White vinegar
   e. Aloe Vera
   f. Tea Tree oil
   g. Turmeric
   h. Peppermint oil and cinnamon
   i. Lavender oil
   j. Chamomile
   k.
3. Burns
   a. Never ice a burn! Immediately place the burned

area under cool running water and use one of the following home remedies for relief:

    i. Aloe Vera
    ii. Mint toothpaste
    iii. Vanilla
    iv. Tea bags
    v. Oats
    vi. Milk and water
    vii. Coconut oil
    viii. Lavender oil
    ix. Honey
    x. Raw potato

4. Low fevers – natural ways to reduce a fever:

    a. Cool water
    b. Basil
    c. Apple cider vinegar
    d. Garlic
    e. Raisins
    f. Ginger

Life Hacks

Using chopsticks

1. Hold your dominant hand loosely. People who clench their chopsticks usually just end up flinging their food all over the place. Place the first chopstick in the valley between your pointer finger and thumb. Balance it on your ring finger.
2. Place the second chopstick in the valley between your pointer finger and thumb along with the first chopstick, but rest this one on your middle finger instead of your ring finger.
3. Use your thumb, pointer and middle fingers to grasp the second chopstick a bit more tightly.
4. The first chopstick (on the bottom) remains more or less stationary. The index and middle fingers do all the heavy lifting with the second chopstick.
5. Using your index and middle fingers to move the top chopstick up and down, open up your chopsticks. And close them over the food. Remember to keep your hand loose but still maintain good control over that chopstick. You'll really be tested when picking up heavier pieces of food. Once you've got a good grip, go ahead and pick it up.

Life Advice

Advice from Rachel

"It's hard to be a leader when no one's following you."
-   Rachel Barnard

"Some girls like to match their panties to their bras, but I like to match my socks to my shirts."
-   Rachel Barnard

"Productivity never stops."
-   Rachel Barnard

"Experience doesn't come with age it comes with life."
-   Rachel Barnard

"Innocence can corrupt power just as easily as power can corrupt innocence."
-   Rachel Barnard

"If you are at peace with yourself you are at peace with the world."
-   Rachel Barnard

"Clothes only define the shape of our bodies, not ourselves."
-   Rachel Barnard

"A perfectionist is not perfect."
-   Rachel Barnard

FASHION FAUX PAS LIST

Nichole's advice for dressing up and going out

- Shoes to avoid: Crocs.
- Trends are great, but you will never be a fashion icon if you're always following someone else.
- Don't wear too many accessories.
- Avoid denim on denim.
- There is such a thing as too much animal print – wear it sparingly!
- Never ever wear socks with sandals!
- Don't let others tell you what to wear.
- Wear your clothes with confidence and people won't question your fashion choices – unless Crocs.
- Always try on something before buying it – sizes lie!
- Shoes will make or break your outfit – so don't blow it!

NICHOLE'S FAVORITE SARASOTA HANGOUTS

- Big E's (2805 N Tamiami Trl.)
- Coffee Carousel (1644 Main St.)
- Selby Library (1331 1st St.)
- Siesta Key Drum Circle (948 Beach Rd, Siesta Key)
- The Starbucks on University (3604 84th ave cir East)
- Hot Tubbing at night (6104 Turnbury Park Dr.)
- Secret Tree Beach (N Shore Rd, Longboat Key)
- The Super Walmart (8320 Lockwood Ridge Rd.)
- The Tab (4141 Desoto Rd.)
- Cat Haven island (5110 San Jose Dr.)
- Downtown Regal Cinemas (1993 Main St.)
- Puppy Town (4045 S Tamiami Trail)
- Munchie's Café (6639 Superior Ave.)
- Unconditional Surrender Sarasota
- New College of FL (5800 Bay Shore Rd.)
- Evie's Golf Course (4735 Bee Ridge Rd.)
- Dog Park (4570 17th St.)

ACKNOWLEDGEMENTS

Thanks to the following sources for their invaluable advice and compilations of common knowledge:

Allrecipes.com

Artofmanliness.com

Bridgestonetire.com

DMV.org

Dummies.com

Startcooking.com

Thewoksoflife.com

Tripadvisor.com

Webmd.com

FOR THE LOVE OF DONUTS BOOKS

Donuts in an Empty Field (For the Love of Donuts Book One)

Letting go of anger is life's greatest challenge.

Vanessa Smith hasn't been the same since her father's death. A hero until the end, he died saving a restaurant owner's wife and son from a burning building. Nessa has always blamed the boy, Ben, for her loss, and her thoughts are consumed with ways to make him as miserable as she is.

Best friend Nichole Adams knows Nessa can never heal until she learns to let go of her hatred, but bringing back her best friend is proving more difficult than she could've imagined. In a last ditch effort to break Nessa's obsession, Nichole hopes signing up for the local food challenge is just the thing to bust her out of her shell.

A single choice defines the road ahead for Nessa. Doing the right thing isn't easy, but living with the consequences of doing nothing might be worse.

FOR THE LOVE OF DONUTS BOOKS

Seize the Donut (For the Love of Donuts Book Two)

Friendships shouldn't be taken for granted.

For Nichole Adams and Vanessa Smith, their friendship has been an unbreakable bond, but high school's over and their lives are moving in different directions.

Vanessa is embarking on her first year at the local college. She's ready to make new friends and leave her past behind. It might be lonely without her bestie, but Vanessa has classes, social activities, and a new group of friends to keep her occupied. And that's before the meet cute with a new guy.

For Nichole, life just isn't going well and Vanessa hasn't been picking up her phone lately. Flirting is much easier for Nichole, but she has much grander problems now, like finding a place to live and getting her car to start each day.

Forever hopeful that things will change, Nichole still clings to the hope that Vanessa will come back to their friendship and be her best friend again.

Something's gotta give and this story of how friendships get off track, lies become reality, and bad luck tails bad choices will bring you in and around the little town of Sarasota, Florida that you grew to love in book one of the series - Donuts in an Empty Field.

DONUTS IN AN EMPTY FIELD
chapter one - Mementos

We haven't opened this room in five years.

"Are you sure you're up for this, Vanessa?" Mom asks.

I nod, but I'm not ready. How can I deal? Dad could be alive if he hadn't tried to be a hero.

I glance back at Mom and take a deep breath before I grab the office doorknob, turn, and push.

The smell hits me. Stale. Musty. Humid.

This is not how I remember Dad.

I hold my breath and look around, trying to recall the distinct way he smelled. This used to be Dad's office. Now it's a stagnant room full of useless things. Things we're going to get rid of. All his books and papers and desk toppers. Junk crammed onto a six-foot desk and packed into a room that is little bigger than a walk in closet.

Mom pats me on the back and I step inside. Letting out a breath with a whoosh, I tiptoe around piles of books on the floor and sit in the office chair. It creaks backwards. Mom stands in the middle of the room with her hands clasped tight together in front of her stomach. Thin streams of sunlight filter through the blinds, highlighting the dust motes in the air.

Bluster noses his way into the room, waddling around to sniff at each pile of books and papers stacked on the floor. I bend down to pet him. Not only is it the anniversary of my father's death, but it's also the anniversary of the day we got Bluster. It's almost as if he came to replace Dad, arriving mere hours ahead of the

incident at the restaurant. Bluster's stubby reddish brown tail beats at my thigh as I try to hold him down and hug him. Bluster's softness rubs against my bare legs. I can hear his heartbeat pattering and his breath wheezing as he struggles to get out of my grip. He smells like a dog should, musty wet from his recent bath. I breathe deep, the smell overpowering the staleness of the office around us.

When Dad brought home Bluster five years ago, I was thrilled. Corgi pups are divine and I was absolutely smitten with the little guy. I'm certain it was the reason boys never interested me until later. From the first tail-wag, mess on the floor, and sharp bark, I was in love.

Mom only shook her head and sighed. Dad was forever surprising both of us with shenanigans. He usually got away with them, too. I dropped hints for years about wanting a dog, but Mom always said no. It was much harder to say "no" to the dog's face.

Bluster and I bonded the minute Dad set him into my arms. No matter how much Mom didn't want a dog, she couldn't take him away from me because Bluster was the last present Dad ever gave me.

Shoes tap in the main part of the house on our wood floors and my best friend Nichole appears in the doorway. She glances at Mom and then locks eyes with me, looking down at me from her model height of 5'8". She hesitates outside the door, still holding my gaze with her own brown eyes. She twirls a slender finger through her shoulder length brown hair with blonde highlights and chews on her lip.

"Are you sure that it's okay for me to be here?" Nichole asks.

I nod and she steps inside, her heels tapping on the

wood floor without rhythm as she takes tentative steps.

"Thank you for coming. Of course it's okay. Vanessa and I very much appreciate you helping out," Mom says.

I frown. "We don't have to do this."

Nichole says at the same time, "It's okay, I wanted to help."

We look at each other. Normally we're more in sync, but today everyone's rhythm is off.

"Thanks, Nichole," I sigh.

She remains silent, waiting for Mom to be the parent and say something helpful.

Mom shakes her head. "It's time." She sighs heavily and unclasps her hands. Mom wears no makeup and her eyelids droop. Her lips are a thin, pale line without lipstick. I have Mom's hair, at least when she was younger, but I don't have to dye mine to keep its dark brunette color.

Nichole purses her lips and I internally roll my eyes at Mom's lack of parental guidance. At the very least, she usually gives me the canned therapy version of sympathy and support, but today is hard for her too.

Mom sweeps her hair over her shoulders, out of her pale face, revealing the too-large ears I inherited. She steps back into the hall to pick up the cleaning supplies we'd forgotten outside the room. Bluster looks up at me and whines. I pet him and he settles down onto the floor.

Touching Dad's precious books and trinkets makes his presence feel closer than it has felt in years, like he could walk in and tell us the corgi bobblehead doesn't belong in a box, but front and center on his desk next to his donut patterned mouse pad. Putting his stuff in a box is like putting him and my memories of him into a box. I

don't want to forget Dad, but both Mom and my therapist agreed it's time to donate the books and clean out the office. That it has to be done. In a single story house with three bedrooms and an office, we sure don't need the space. I don't understand why today, of all days it has to be done, but it isn't my choice. Mom wants to get it over with. She has plans tomorrow. I don't have enough energy to object.

"So," Nichole says into the silence. "I'm glad you have the air-conditioning on, it's hot out there." She wipes the back of her hand over her forehead. Her cheeks are sun-tanned, slightly darker than her normal olive skin tone. We're both of mixed European heritage, but Nichole got genes for tanning and I didn't.

"It's Florida in the summer. Of course it's hot," I say. I get up out of the office chair, releasing a puff of dust.

Mom starts with the pictures. Photos clutter Dad's desk and windowsill, overlapping with smiles and memories. My heart constricts tighter and tighter with every photo placed face down in one of the medium-sized boxes Mom dragged in. I don't want to cry in front of Nichole. If I'm too much of a bother, she might leave and hang out with her other friends, doing something more fun.

The sun creates shadows through the dusty blinds, striping on the box like a jail cell. I apologize silently to Dad's memory as I nestle in each new photo.

"Do you want to keep any, Vanessa?" Mom asks.

I look at the collection of bobble heads on his desk, the Rubik's cubes and desktop puzzles, the office toys. They don't remind me of Dad the way Bluster does. They don't mean more than my memories of him. I shake my head at Mom and she tilts her head, regarding

me, before settling back into the routine of placing odds and ends from the desk into boxes.

Then I see the last photograph.

It's a larger picture, printed at home and tacked onto the corkboard in a hurry. On Dad's last day alive, after he'd surprised me with the dog, he took us to Sarasota's only dog park. Bluster was six months old, still small enough for me to hold him tight to my chest without his legs falling out of my arms, but old enough to mingle with the park's smaller dogs. We'd gone to the dog park to let Bluster socialize and Dad was going to break the world record for most powdered donuts eaten in three minutes. After Bluster wore himself out, we put him back on the leash and left the dog area to find ourselves a secluded picnic table.

The picture was taken after Dad failed. Powdered sugar coated Dad's beard, the top of Bluster's head, even dusting the park bench and floating to the ground below. Mom kept trying to wipe powdered sugar off Dad's beard.

Dad had no qualms asking a stranger to take our photo. It was frustrating that I couldn't even remember if the stranger had been a man or a woman.

I remember Dad.

Dad was an inch or two above average height, about 6 feet tall, and had the regular dad paunch that signifies the presence of children who never finish their own dinner and give leftovers to Dad to eat. He was always trying to talk or wave to strangers. Everyone always recognized Dad for his friendliness. I wonder if it was to show me that good people exist in the world. That I could be one of them.

I reach up to pull the photo off the corkboard, but

my hand stops halfway. I can't do it. This is still Dad's office, in some way, and the picture belongs here.

Mom smiles at the picture, but her eyes still droop and her lips are so thin they almost disappear into her mouth.

"It'll get better," Mom says.

"You still have each other," Nichole offers. "And you have me," she adds.

"I know."

"This is really hard for both of us." Mom looks away. "I've scheduled you with Dr. Bryan later today while I'm out with Walter."

"Your new boyfriend, right?" Nichole asks.

Mom won't meet my gaze. I know this is hard for her, too. I try to give her a break for setting up a dating profile online. For abandoning me on the hardest weekend of the year for a date. I'm mad at her for being so open about dating again, for telling me about it and expecting me to accept that she's moved on when I haven't.

"Walter has been helping me get through this, too."

Nichole looks at me for an explanation, but I don't want to get into the argument about Mom dating again right now.

"I'm kind of hungry, Mrs. S.," Nichole says, sensing our discomfort.

Mom nods absently.

"How 'bout a snack Mrs. Smith," Nichole says louder.

Mom shakes her head as if to clear away her thoughts. "Sure, be right back girls."

Nichole waits until Mom's out of the room to start

shoving books into another larger box.

"Hey," I say.

Nichole pauses and stands up straight to regard me. "What? You're dragging this out and it's not going to get easier the longer you do it. Let's get it over with."

Nichole walks over to me, reaches up to grab the photograph off the wall and I slap her arm away.

"Seriously? Come on Vanessa."

"Don't you dare. You can't just walk in here and throw his stuff into boxes like it's junk."

Nichole raises her eyebrows and takes a step back.

"That's not what I-"

"I'm going to leave this one," I say with a scowl.

Nichole holds up her hands in surrender.

"Fine," she says.

I reach up to touch the photograph, fingering one of the loose corners at the bottom. Peripherally I see Nichole take another step back, watching the wall and my finger.

She trips over a stack of books on the floor. I don't think. Swiveling to help her, my finger is still hooked around the edge of the picture. It rips as I leap sideways to grab at Nichole's flailing arms. She backpedals over the stack of books. I yank her back to the open floor and let go of her arm. The ripped corner of the photo clutched in my fingers flutters to the ground.

Nichole sucks in a breath as I turn to face the ruined picture. Something flutters behind the missing corner and I lift the stiff paper to peer behind it.

Something is there.

Nichole and I both jump at the sound of a crash from

the front of the house.

"Mom!" I yell.

I'm wound up from being in Dad's office, from remembering our last day together, to the finality of packing up his stuff that I go into panic mode and run toward the door. Nichole bumps into me in our haste to make sure Mom's okay and we both fall to the floor. My world turns upside down and I bang my head against Nichole's knee. I'm panting and scrambling to disentangle my limbs from Nichole's. Mom still hasn't answered.

We run out to see what happened. Mom's in the kitchen, her hands braced on opposite sides of the sink. For a moment I'm immensely angry that she didn't answer when I called, scaring the bejesus out of Nichole and me, but then I notice she's crying. Shame at my anger crashes down on my shoulders.

"Give us a minute?" I ask Nichole.

She nods and heads back to the office. I wince at the sounds of books smacking into one other as Nichole throws them into boxes.

"Mom?"

"It just slipped," she says without looking up.

Several large pieces of one of our flowered yellow and green plates are on the ground next to Mom. We've never broken any of the plates before.

Thankfully, I'm wearing my favorite pair of Crocs, and I don't have to leave Mom alone right now to go get shoes. I can see smaller pieces of the ceramic littering the floor in between tufts of Bluster's fur and crumbs from our last meal.

"It's okay, Mom."

I bend in to hug her and she turns to me with shaking shoulders, sniffling and blinking to stop her tears.

"It'll get easier," I tell her, patting her on the back.

"Grief is a funny thing. It's never the same and it's always a tough upward climb, but you'll get there. It won't be easy, but you're strong and you'll get through it," Mom assures me, turning back into the parent.

Ugh. There's the canned therapy talk. At least she's feeling more like herself, even if I don't.

I notice she doesn't include herself in the statement.

"Don't you miss him?"

"Of course I miss him; he was your father." She sighs out.

The anger knots tight, pressed up against the agony and emptiness Dad left behind. He wasn't just my father; he was Mom's husband. He had friends. He was a part of my world and now he's pictures and mementos and everything I still remember about him, and more that I can't.

I don't want to replace Dad, but I want to move on. I put on a brave face, masking my emotions as best I can and say, "Nichole and I can take care of the rest of Dad's stuff."

"Thank you, Vanessa," Mom agrees.

Dad wouldn't have wanted me to get upset at Mom, especially since she's also sad today. I grab her shoes for her. She smiles at me with another sigh.

"You go ahead with Nichole. I'm going to clean this up first. Here." Mom hands me a bag of carrots and some homemade hummus. "For Nichole and for you if you get hungry." She glances at my stomach tight against my shirt and I suck in reflexively. Even on this bad day,

she has to remind me that I'm overweight.

I take the snack and walk back to the office. Nichole sits in the chair, using her feet to swivel herself back and forth as she holds something in her hands.

"What, break time already?" I ask. The anger knots tighter.

Nichole drops the piece of paper onto the desk and I can't help but watch is it flutters back and forth before settling off-kilter near the edge.

"What does it say?" I ask.

"I don't know." Nichole hands it to me. It's a lined notebook paper with a bunch of scribbles. Sorrow hits me. I don't recognize the handwriting, but it has his name at the top, under the date.

The numbers blur as I hold back the tears. I've forgotten another part of my memories of Dad.

I read through the scribbles and turn to Nichole in confusion. I show her the note.

July 22, 2002
1. ~~Get a dog~~
2. Win a food challenge.
3. Shoot a gun.
4. Ride a motorcycle.
5. Skydive.
6. Perform a kind deed without expecting anything in return.

"It's a bucket list," she explains.

"But why?"

"What do you mean, why? Most people have them,"

Nichole says.

"Not my dad. He would have told me."

Nichole gives me a funny look. "Seems like your dad though. I mean, c'mon, win a food challenge?"

"Yeah, it does kind of sound like him. But only one has been crossed out." I frown, thinking of everything Dad never got a chance to accomplish. Did he even get a chance to try half of these things? "The day he died." I gulp and close my eyes for a long blink. "The day he died, he was trying to beat the world record for most donuts eaten in three minutes. I remember that day. Almost every detail. Why isn't that on this list, why the generic food challenge?"

Nichole doesn't answer and I continue. "He took us, Mom, Bluster and I to the dog park. He was always into getting things done. A dog and donuts on the same day, in the same place. I remember he let me hold the timer. It made me feel important."

Nichole nods.

"He wasn't very good at eating donuts fast, but he made us laugh. He was covered in powdered sugar and it made me think of Christmas snow. I was proud and embarrassed for Dad at the same time. He was so fun, but he was always doing weird things."

Nichole inclines her head at my words and gets out of the office chair. She paces the room twice and then starts methodically and carefully putting books into boxes.

"I remember I could taste the powdered sugar. He was eating so fast that it was poofing everywhere. Bluster kept winding his leash under his legs as he watched us. Mom and I both laughed at Dad. He managed to swallow the first donut and was already stuffing the

second one into his mouth."

I stop my story and sigh. Nichole looks up at me.

"I'm listening," she says.

"There was no way he was going to beat the record and I teased him the rest of the day for failing. Now, I wish I hadn't." I look down at my hands, Dad's bucket list clenched in them.

"You should do it," Nichole declares.

"What?"

"You should do his bucket list."

"What? No way."

Mom appears in the doorway. I slide the paper under a stack of folders on the desk.

"Everything alright?" she asks.

Nichole looks at me and I shrug.

"Here, I'll take the boxes out to the car," she offers.

She lifts one of the heavier, book-filled boxes and staggers out. I'm glad we're donating his books, but I'm sad to see them go. The room is empty without them.

"Are you going to tell her about the list?" Nichole asks.

I consider it. "No. I don't think so." I don't want to share this piece of Dad with anyone else. Mom would make me share it with my therapist. She would minimize it and then disappear on a date.

"Well, I'm pooped. Do you want me to stick around?" Nichole asks.

"Ugh no, Mom scheduled a session for me later this afternoon. Why can't she just pull me out of class like all the other parents so I can at least skip school?" The humor sounds foreign to my ears because I'm still reeling

from cleaning out Dad's office and having to comfort Mom.

I retrieve the list from under the files and walk up to take down the photograph from the corkboard. I want to move on. Nichole ushers me out of the room, clutching the unopened bag of carrots, Bluster following behind us. I clutch both the bucket list and the ripped photograph in my hands as she shuts the door firmly behind us.

SEIZE THE DONUT
Chapter one

Where *are you?* Nichole texted her best friend, Vanessa, her fingers stabbing at the keys. Nichole was terrified that Sharon, her mom, might discover Johnny's wallet. The wallet he couldn't find after their extravagant meal just minutes ago. Nichole had to fork over the cash, every second pushing her further and further into panic.

It had seemed like such a wild idea to do it on her mom's bed. Where else could the wallet possibly end up? Sharon would flip if she found the wallet, not only because of where it was, but because of what was on it.

Nichole shifted her weight nervously from foot to foot and chewed on one of her fingernails, tasting the bitterness of the nail polish in her mouth. Her blonde-streaked hair caught on the jagged edge of her fingernail as she pulled her fingers through it. The messy ponytail she'd artfully put together before the date was loose and knotted.

Vanessa was late. Again. It'd been happening more and more as Vanessa got ready to go to college and didn't pay as much attention to Nichole as she used to. Ever since the incident at Booker High School several months ago, Vanessa had been growing distant again. Quieter. Like she was before they became friends and Nichole brought her out of her shell.

Nichole stared up at the blinking gas station sign with resignation. She didn't want to walk home in these shoes. Her wedges were great for her date with Johnny, but terrible for the poorly maintained Florida sidewalks. Besides, Vanessa promised to be here. The muggy early evening air pressed on her and she wiped beads of sweat

from her face.

Nichole's phone buzzed and then the ringer sang out one of Eminem's rap refrains, loud and echoing in the warm Sarasota evening air. Nichole pushed "call" so hard the phone slipped out of her hand and she had to fumble to catch it before it fell to the ground.

"Where are you?" Nichole yelped.

"So sorry," Vanessa said.

"Vanessa!" Nichole said in complete exasperation. Nichole kicked a toe into the pavement and stared daggers at some dude who immediately looked away from her chest as he went into the 7-11. She noted with dismay that she'd smeared grit into the toe her wedges.

"I'm like ten minutes away. I'll be right there, chill," Vanessa replied.

"Just hurry up, okay?" Nichole pleaded.

"Going as fast as I can," Vanessa said.

Nichole punched "end." She shouldn't be taking her frustration out on Vanessa, but it was hard to keep her growing panic to herself. A woman exiting the 7-11 wrinkled her nose at Nichole and steered wide around her. Nichole stood, leaning against the side of the building for another ten minutes, anxiously peering around for Vanessa's Honda Civic. She slid to the ground in dismay, not caring if she got her short shorts and halter top dirty. After another ten minutes, Vanessa pulled up and flashed her lights.

Nichole rocketed up, accidentally slammed the car door as she got in.

"Sorry, Mom made me clean up after Bluster," Vanessa said. "He puked all over the rug."

Nichole crossed her arms after strapping on her seat belt.

"Why couldn't Johnny drop you off?" Vanessa asked, pulling onto the road.

"I already told you. Mom doesn't like Johnny."

"So?" Vanessa said.

"Well," Nichole said, looking away from her bestie. "I, uh, never told you but Johnny's a bit older than me."

Vanessa glanced briefly at Nichole before returning to driving.

"I didn't want you to worry," Nichole added.

"Nichole, how long have we been friends?" Vanessa asked.

"Four years. Ever since the beginning of high school."

"Exactly. I thought you were done keeping me out of the loop."

The unspoken words, "since last year" echoed in Nichole's mind, making her wince. Yes, she'd fudged the truth to Vanessa when they were seniors in high school, but she'd eventually come clean. Besides, it was for Vanessa's own good.

Nichole glanced briefly toward Vanessa's upper leg where she'd been grazed by a bullet just months ago when that little lie had caused major consequences.

"You're right. I shouldn't have. Can you go any faster?"

"Why are you in such a hurry?" Vanessa asked.

Nichole chewed on her fingernail and shifted in her seat. "Johnny left his wallet at my house."

"So. No big deal."

Nichole's right foot pressed down as if she could

make the car accelerate.

"You can tell me," Vanessa insisted.

"He's 29."

"Shut up!" Vanessa exclaimed.

"Yeah."

"No wonder your mom doesn't like him."

"She doesn't know!" Nichole said vehemently.

"You sure about that? Where's his wallet?"

Nichole sighed. "I don't know. It, uh, might be in her bed."

"No!" Vanessa said.

"Yes."

"You should have told me. I would have come sooner."

Nichole shook her head. "You had to take care of Bluster. I understand."

"I came as soon as I was done."

"I can tell. What are you wearing, anyway? That shirt is past your knees," Nichole said.

"It's my corgi shirt and he looks just like Bluster," Vanessa insisted

Vanessa always wore baggy clothes, but this one was like an ill-fitting dress. It was too big, even for a nightshirt.

"I only wear it around the house. And I know it's way too baggy and I know you're always telling me I don't have to wear baggy clothes."

"Well, fashion aside, I'm glad you came as soon as you did. I know how long it can take you to make dressing decisions."

Vanessa smiled as they turned into their neighborhood. "You ready? What if your mom found

it?"

"She would have sent Lewis to come get me."

"Your mom's harsh, but not that bad," Vanessa protested as she pulled into Nichole's driveway.

"It's been getting worse all summer. She's been on my case to do something and work harder and clean my room. She can't even clean the house and she expects me to clean my room!"

Vanessa glanced over and narrowed her eyes. "Don't chew on your fingernails," she said.

Nichole pulled her finger from her lips and looked out the window.

"Whatever happens, you can stay at my house tonight, deal?" Vanessa said.

Nichole nodded her head, her eyes focused on the closed front door of her house. She got out slowly. Before she could take two steps from the Civic, Sharon burst through the door and threw something small at Nichole. It hit her square in the chest and bounced to the ground. A familiar red Rolling Stones sticker stared back at her.

"You lied to us!" Sharon barked.

Nichole bent down to pick up Johnny's wallet.

"Don't ignore me, Nichole. And you!" Sharon pointed a threatening finger at Vanessa who shrunk into herself as if her shirt was a security blanket. "You are a bad influence."

Vanessa glanced back at Nichole and took a step back toward the car.

"This is my house. I don't care that you're 18. When you live in my house, you live by my rules. I will not have my daughter dating someone more than 10 years older than her! What they hell were you thinking?"

"Mom," Nichole pleaded.

"Don't 'Mom' me!" Sharon said, holding up a hand. "You've gone behind my back enough. I don't know how you got involved with that boy at Booker, but now you've lied straight to my face about Jerry!"

"Johnny," Nichole corrected, her eyes narrowing.

Sharon threw up her hands. "How do you know he's not married? Hm? He could have any number of STDs! It didn't escape my notice that I found his wallet under my bed."

"Calm down, Mom!" Nichole shouted. She stepped closer to Sharon, jutting her chin out in defiance. She was still an inch shorter than her mother, so she placed her hands on her hips and glared."

"Why can't you go to college like Vanessa and meet a nice college boy?" Sharon said. "Someone closer to your age?"

Vanessa gasped behind Nichole.

"I don't have to take this. Like you said, I'm over 18. I'm an adult," Nichole shouted.

"Not in my house!" Sharon shouted back.

"Fine, then I won't stay in your house. I'll move in with Johnny. And he's only 29!" Nichole yelled.

"What!" Sharon spluttered.

"You want me out? Then I'm out and I won't be coming back." Nichole stared over at Vanessa. "Come on Ness, let's get out of here."

Vanessa opened and closed her mouth several times before following mutely to the car and getting in.

"But," Vanessa said.

"Just drive," Nichole said, crossing her arms over her chest like a second seat belt. "I'm not coming back until she's gone," she added.

Vanessa backed out of the drive and idled in the street for a moment.

"Just go!" Nichole cried.

Vanessa gunned it and the car screeched off down the road.

"I don't like this," Vanessa said after they'd left their neighborhood behind.

Nichole sighed, her thoughts jumbling into one cohesive thought.

Johnny.

He was older, he would know what to do.

"I can stay with Johnny," Nichole said. "I'm sorry you had to be there. You're okay, right?"

"Yeah, I can't believe Sharon yelled at you like that."

"It's been a long time coming. We've been arguing for months. Whatever."

"Are you sure Johnny's the best choice?" Vanessa asked.

"Not you too!" Nichole blurted, sitting up straight in her seat.

"Don't take this the wrong way, but you barely talk about him and you just told me how old he is. You've only been dating for a month. Are you sure he's the right one?"

"I didn't want you to worry. After Ben and graduating and you going off to college, I didn't want to create problems that weren't problems. And we've been dating for almost six weeks."

"And yet here you are. You don't even have a toothbrush or a car," Vanessa pointed out.

Nichole slumped in the seat in defeat. "I'm taking my car. It was my present after all. I'll have Johnny drive me back tonight when Mom's out at her shift. Lewis is almost never home."

"Okay, it's your life. I don't like it, but I'm here

for you."

"Thanks, Ness. I owe you."

"I'm still paying you back for saving my life, even though you lied about my Dad's bucket list. I'd call it even."

"Don't even start on the bucket list thing again! I only lied about it because it was for your own good," Nichole said vehemently.

"Have to keep you on your toes. And FYI, it's only been a couple of months," Vanessa said. "And besides," Vanessa emphasized the word dramatically. "You A wrote a fake bucket list, B stashed it where I'd find it and think it was my Dad's, and C only told me the truth after months had gone by and Ben nearly shot us."

"I get it. I get it." Nichole held up her hands in surrender and Vanessa smiled.

"So, where are we going exactly?" Vanessa asked.

"He's South by the Westfield."

"Nichole! That's like Osprey!"

"Please?"

With a sigh, Vanessa nodded her head and made a U-turn, heading down to I-75. Nichole's hands shook the closer they got to South Sarasota. What if Johnny didn't want her to stay?

OTHER BOOKS BY RACHEL BARNARD

At One's Beast
Young Adult
Fairy Tale Adaptation
Low Fantasy
Love Triangle
Available in print, e-book, and as an audiobook

Wandering Imagination
A small book of poems that almost got away.

Ataxia and the Ravine of Lost Dreams
Young Adult
Dystopian
Action & Adventure
A hint of Romance
A bit of Science Fiction.
Available in print, e-book, and as an audiobook.

AT ONE'S BEAST BY RACHEL BARNARD

From once upon a time to happily ever after, At One's Beast highlights the struggles of two young adolescents who have fallen prey to chance evil circumstances. When it took the entire village to create the monster, what will it take to break the spell?

Available in print, e-book, and as an audio book, At One's Beast is a new take on "Beauty and the Beast," with a love triangle, revenge, a spell, evil, fate, forgiveness, compassion, bitterness, capture, betrayal and love.

ATAXIA AND THE RAVINE OF LOST DREAMS BY RACHEL BARNARD

In Ataxia and the Ravine of Lost Dreams A young girl takes on the mighty powers of the government but is sidetracked by challenges of the academy she attends, the new boy, and keeping her secrets safe.

She will do anything - forfeit her identity, friendships, even love - to be humanity's champion.

As the U.S. government prepares to take over the world, MC infiltrates one of their elite academies that trains future leaders. MC must rise to the top in the Cube training grounds in order to be placed high up within the government so she can stop it in its takeover.

It is not until her fourth and final year at the academy that her top-student status is threatened by the sudden arrival of Li, the new transfer student. MC is completely focused on her self-created mission until she gets sidetracked by Li, who might be bad news in more ways than which she bargained.

A Young Adult, Dystopian, Not-So-Distant-Future Adventure Novel with a hint of sci-fi and a bit of romance.

ABOUT THE AUTHOR

I am an author
I am a geocacher
I am an ice cream lover
I am efficient
I am an idea generator
I am impatient
I am loyal
I am hazel eyed
I am a wearer of fuzzy socks
I am a Pinewood Derby and Boot Tossing Winner
I am someone with stage fright
I am learning
I am color coding my calendar
I am clever
I am a blogger
I am a reader
I am an Indie supporter
I am a dancer
I am compiling and listing and analyzing
I am not a fish

Favorite word: sesquipedalian
Favorite type of donut: glazed
Favorite movie: Wedding Singer
Favorite scent: sleep
Favorite item to collect: Chapstick
Favorite fruit: peach

Dear Future Self,

It is the year 2027. You finally finished writing your 50th novel. Will you ever say no to any challenge? You always have to one-up your dad. SMH. You probably don't even know what that acronym means anymore! You're so old! By the way, Dad's series has become a hit and you get to cameo in the upcoming movie.

Donuts are out of fashion now, so it's all about the bagels. Just kidding! Croissant donuts are still going strong and they've even developed a new fad: donut pops (they're the new cake pop). You might open up a shop and sell them for a few months until you get bored.

Florida finally got hit with an insane hurricane named Vanessa (coincidence?) that wiped out many of the locations you based your scenes on in the Donuts Books. So sad, but at least the rebuilding efforts are going well and you have a new project to focus on.

Now what are you going to do?

Sincerely,

Rachel Barnard   3/31/17
From the Future

www.ingramcontent.com/pod-product-compliance
Lightning Source LLC
Chambersburg PA
CBHW051046030426
42339CB00006B/224